A Sideline Guide to Boys Lacrosse

Written By David Wilbur
Illustrated By Kevin Wilbur

Published in America by Writers Room Books,
4 W. Oakland Avenue, Doylestown, PA, 18901.

Edited by Ben Cake

Printed by Thomson-Shore, Inc., Dexter, Michigan.

ISBN 0-9747191-0-2

To Walt, with gratitude

Table of Contents

Introduction

THE OLDEST game in America, lacrosse is becoming the next new thing. According to a 2002 survey, membership to *USLacrosse*, the national governing body of lacrosse, is growing in some areas as fast as 40% per year. Each year, there are over 20,000 new players with, more or less, 40,000 newly confused parents.

Lacrosse is derived from a game called Tewaarathon or Dehonchigwiis, "the little brother of war," played across North America by indigenous people. The game had many variations. Goals were often makeshift. In some versions, the object was to hit a tree with the ball, in others, to cross a line. Field size varied according to terrain. Sticks and nets came in a wide range of styles. Games were played for short periods or for days.

The game was also a preparation for participation in war. Drums inaugurated a match and accompanied the players to the field. Paint and feathers were worn. Ceremony and ritual in praise of the Creator were observed. Formality preceded the mayhem of a match. Today, the point of the game, to instill community and spirituality into young men, while testing their athletic prowess, remains constant and much of the flavor for the old game remains.

In northern New York state, among the Oneida

Indians and in lower Canada around Montreal, whites first encountered the game. Demonstrations were given and the game caught on with the new people. The settlers of French descent named it "La Crosse" from the shape of the stick and its head. In the mid-1800's lacrosse rules became formalized. By the latter part of the century, in typicaly colonial style, Indians were banned from the leagues.

From such beginnings, the game has evolved into a worldwide phenomenon. Countries as remote from its origins as the Czech Republic, South Korea and Scotland now have leagues and players passionate about the game.

This pocket-sized guide to the sport of men's lacrosse is designed to meet the needs of the parent of a lacrosse player. In clear and concise terms, with accompanying illustrations, the goal of this book is to provide answers to the common parental sideline query, "What in the world just happened?"

The game combines speed, deft coordination, open space, special equipment, and controlled aggression. These are elements tailor-made to appeal to young men. Additionally, there is the delight in playing a game of which one's parents typically know nothing about. This book hopes to provide a remedy for that situation.

In reading this book, please note that, while every effort has been made to provide accurate information, the book may become outdated or local conditions may affect elements such as the field size or the length of play. Also keep in mind that, as the game is growing in popularity, the number of available, well-trained and experienced coaches and referees is diminishing. There are not enough to go around. Use this book, then, not as a standard but as a guide to the rules and regulations.

The book begins with some thoughts on the sport from one parent to another, including notes on safety. Then, there is a short discussion regarding the culture of the game followed by specifics on the elements of the game, including field of play, equipment, and personnel. The start of the game is explained and then the course of play with penalties and special situations discussed in context. The book is best read from start to finish as terms are introduced along the way.

The general format of this guide is to show an illustration, give a brief description of what is happening and offer some possibilities for any penalties or events that may seem unclear. Game situations do not always follow the ideal and there may be deficiencies in the guide. Personalities can come into play and severity is a qualitative characteristic. Do not assume that an official is wrong because the guide suggests something else. Follow up after the match with a coach and learn more.

One final caution is in order. Lacrosse is a beautiful game, at the same time exciting, skillful and extraordinary. Novices and experienced parents alike can gain most from watching and enjoying rather than worrying about nuances. Sometimes it is enough to leave things unexplained.

From one Parent to Another: A Few Things to Note about Lacrosse

Game Preparation

LACROSSE IS not a game normally canceled due to weather. Standing on the sidelines can be a great way to get hypothermia. Dress warmly and stay as dry as possible. On the other extreme, a lacrosse game or tournament can be a wonderful opportunity to get too much sun. Wear a hat and use sun guard.

Bathrooms are not often found anywhere near a lacrosse field. If you don't want to miss any of the action looking for one, avoid that second cup of coffee, or drink it during the game, not before.

Success

GETTING YOUR child to practices and games early and always will greatly increase his chances of success. The best players spend hour after hour practicing. You can help. Have a catch with your child (use a baseball glove if you can't manage a lacrosse stick), or drive him to someplace with a wall to bounce against or a goal to shoot at.

Lacrosse equipment is not cheap. The better the equipment, however, the better the level of play and safety. While you shouldn't skimp on equipment, you don't have to turn your nose up to the idea of buying used equipment, either. Quality does not diminish with use and hand-me-downs are a godsend.

Living with Lacrosse

LACROSSE BALLS and sticks do not live easily with nice furniture, electronic equipment, windows and bric-a-brac. At a minimum, keep the balls out of the house. This will be a never-ending battle.

Tournaments, camps, and clubs all produce large amounts of paraphenalia. Some say the stuff breeds. Don't be surprised when your home begins to accumulate jackets, pinnies, visors and towels, all sporting logos of various lacrosse organizations, many of which your player has never attended. It is an unstoppable phenomenon. It is best just to accept it. A shovel or pitchfork may come in handy on laundry day.

Young men engaged in energetic activities produce a remarkable level of stink. Most players consider it bad luck to wash their pads and uniforms during the season. If you value your olfactory senses, you may want to purchase an equipment bag. Don't be foolish enough to open it indoors during the season.

Some Thoughts about Spectator Safety

LACROSSE IS a rough game played with hard sticks and a very hard ball. Watching a game can be quite dangerous to spectators that do not pay attention or know what to look for. To ensure your own safety, make note of the following:

The ball is hard. Keep your eye on it at all times. If you are having a catch with your child, do not look away when he has the ball and do not throw it until you are sure he is looking at you.

While arriving for a game or a tournament, be alert to players warming up or fooling around. There is rarely any safe distance between the spectators and the players and if your hands are full of folding chairs, small children and camera equipment, it can be tough to react.

Be aware of what is behind you while you are having a catch. The ball will break a window or dent an automobile in an instant. So, watch where you park. A hard shot and a bad bounce will travel 50 yards easily.

Being on the sidelines during a game is the best way to enjoy lacrosse. However, if you are going to be on the sidelines, stand. Do not sit. The game can come your way very quickly and, unlike the players, you are not young, fit and dressed in helmet and pads. You need to be able to get out of the way, sometimes in a hurry.

If you are minding other children or you need to sit during the game, move at least fifteen feet away from the sidelines. Do not read a book, even this one, during play. Keep alert.

Be extremely cautious while filming a lacrosse match or taking pictures before and after a game. If players are in the vicinity and are warming up, you are in danger. Use your head and a long lens.

Ice and ice packs are very good first aid items. Help your son's team by making sure that they are well prepared for injury.

If your son is color blind, be certain that the coach is aware. Use white balls, as yellow balls may blend into the scenery for such a player. The yellow balls are harder to find in the grass and harder to see against the trees. Red balls are invisible to a color blind player.

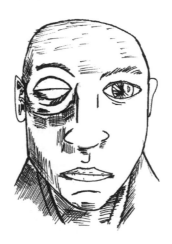

This game is heavy in testosterone and the competition often becomes heated. Fistfights can occur. Stay out of it. The game is for the players, referees and coaches. Not for you. You are there to cheer, commiserate and chauffeur. Let them go. If it gets out of hand, you and your son walk off until things are sorted out.

A Career in Lacrosse

LACROSSE IS a fraternity and lacrosse players share a bond. Your son is a member of this club the first day he steps on the field. Older players help younger players, sometimes a little roughly, and everyone knows everyone else. It is usual and common to see opponents on the field having conversations when the play is not coming their way.

The inclusive nature of the sport manifests itself in many ways, some quite surprising in today's sports-crazed world. For instance, the stars of the game, past and present, are very approachable. It is a rare thing to see a star turn his back on a young player. Normally, the biggest stars go well beyond the call of duty when giving their time and attention to the up-and-comers.

With everyone talking to one another, however, a sort of ruthless peer pressure is exerted. Players and coaches with hot tempers are well known. Dirty or selfish players are acknowledged and anticipated. Reputations, good and bad, are made and last a long time. A good piece of advice from a parent to a young player would suggest that the opponent they face today may, one day in the future, end up a teammate. So, behave accordingly.

A successful career in lacrosse typically entails picking up the game anywhere from age 7 to 15, playing in a municipal league, then high school. The player will then attend a college offering an opportunity to play, will graduate, take a job and join a men's club to continue to play until age 50 or so. If, along the way, the player becomes a parent in their own right, they will participate in the youth program as a coach or a referee.

As with other sports, there are different levels of participation. The highest levels include all-star clubs and elite tournaments, state championships and division-1 and division-3 colleges. Beyond that, there are professional lacrosse leagues, both indoor and outdoor. These leagues resemble the old professional football league, in that, the majority of participants hold down regular jobs, as well. Lacrosse is not an easy sport with which to try to make a living.

Everyone is impressed by the all-star organizations, in awe of the state championship high school teams and dreams of playing for the five or six best college teams. Truth be told, however, they are also content just to play. The passion for the game does not diminish according to the level of the play and at least in college, the highest levels can be a distraction to the more serious business of obtaining a degree. Lacrosse players graduate, keep in touch, and tend to hire one another.

To help your son immerse himself in the culture of lacrosse, encourage him to watch older players, attend college games, and if possible, go to the NCAA championships each spring. Convince his club to enter tournaments, even if the team is seriously overmatched. Along with constant practice, the best way to improve is by playing against good players. Try to get him to attend one of the better camps, such as the ones held at Syracuse or Virginia (see Camps, p.92). His play will grow in leaps and bounds and he will get to know excellent players and coaches.

Before the Game

Field Layout

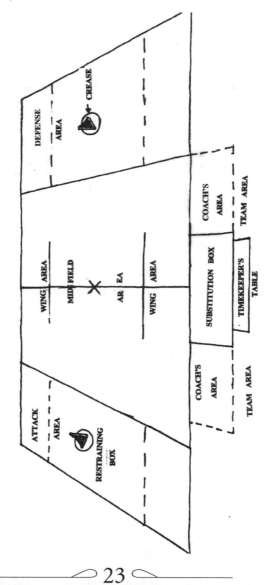

THE PLAYING field is 110 yards long and 60 yards wide. There is a boxed area on each end of the field. The box is 35 yards long and 40 yards wide and 10 yards away from the sideline on each side.

For each team, the field is broken into a defensive area, a midfield, and an attack area. In the midfield area, there are two wing areas that are 20 yards away from the center point on the field.

The goal line is 15 yards away from the end line and 20 yards away from the end of the box. The goal crease must have a radius of 9 feet from the mid-point of the goal line.

On one sideline, is a coaching area followed by the substitution box then the opponent's coaching area. Behind each coach's area is the team area, where players who are not in the game must stand. Behind the substitution box there is the timekeeper's table.

Parents and spectators are normally on the other side of the field from the teams, and are encouraged to stay there. Teams who have "their act together" will provide a scoreboard at a far corner within sight of all the spectators.

Equipment

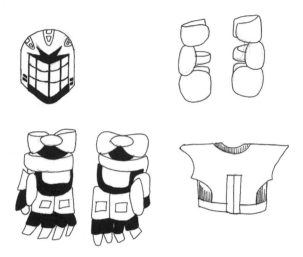

FOR PLAYERS, lacrosse equipment becomes an obsession, and much discussion and time is spent on it. Expect money to be spent just as liberally. While just how far you go is left up to the individual, there are basic requirements.

Each player must wear the following equipment: a helmet, a type of chest/shoulder pad, pair of elbow pads and gloves. A mouth guard must be worn at all times. Failing to keep a mouth guard in one's mouth is a penalty, even if a collision knocks it free. In addition, all helmet straps must be fastened at all times. Loose equipment will result in a warning from the referee. Repeated warnings result in a penalty.

An athletic protector (crotch cup) is not required by rule but anyone hoping to remain healthy will wear one. Even with a cup on, there is little pain to compare to stopping a shot or a stick in the crotch area. Most players would rather break a bone.

In some leagues, there are regulations about uniform color and the size of numbers on the jerseys. Mouthpieces must be a solid color and underwear, protective or not, must be white or gray. Violations can entail warnings or personal fouls depending on the league rules and the opinion of the officials.

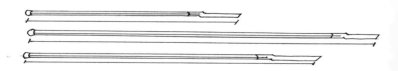

A mid-fielder and attack's stick (crosse) must be between 40 to 42 inches in length. A defensive crosse (long pole) must be between the lengths of 52 to 72 inches. The goalie stick's length can vary between 40 to 72 inches.

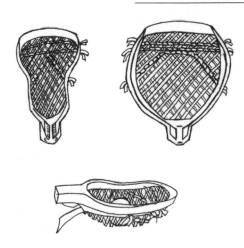

The dimensions of a head is 6 ½ inches at its widest point and with a length of 10 inches from the top of the head to the beginning of the base of the head. A goalie's head must be 10 to 12 inches wide and have a length that cannot exceed 16 ½ inches.

The pocket of the head of a lacrosse stick is woven by hand using different types of strings. The strings that run down the sides and attach to the head are called the "side-wall" strings. The strings running across the pocket are the "shooting" strings. The remaining strings make up the "mesh." A typical mesh is the 10-diamond variety.

Players will see that their stick head is strung according to their preference. Learning to string a crosse is one of the initiation rites of lacrosse. Newly strung heads need to be broken in. A player should never use a newly strung stick in a game. Embarrassing results may occur.

Now and then, a stringing is found to be illegal by an official. A pocket is considered illegal when a person can see any amount of light above the ball when it is in the pocket and the stick is held flat at eye level. Gloves can be deemed illegal if the palms are cut out for better grip.

If equipment is suspected to be illegal, an opposing coach may ask the official to check it. This can backfire as it usually irritates the other team, sometimes to the point of markedly improving play. It is not unusual for a coach to call for inspection of a stick, have the stick deemed legal by the officials and have the owner of the stick immediately score a goal with it.

The Players

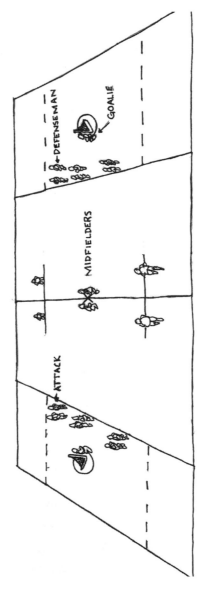

A LACROSSE team on the field consists of a goalie, three defense players, three mid-field players and three attack players. On the sidelines, there is usually a coach and enough substitutes to maintain a high level of play. Good teams have a goalie coach, a defense coach, a mid-field coach and an attack coach. They field three or four mid-field lines and two attack lines.

During play, most teams field a long-pole mid-fielder during face-offs and in defensive situations, switching to a short-pole mid-fielder when in the attack. This mode of play explains the constant running on and off the field of the mid-fielders. When done properly, the pace of play is not affected. For most teams below the college level, it can seem to be chaotic. No more than four long-poles per team may be on the field at once.

Some mid-fielders specialize in defense and some are better attuned to attack. Once again, as with the long-pole mid-fielder, substitutions meant to ensure the proper personnel are on the field for each situation can result in confusion. Younger players do not specialize and are usually substituted based on exhaustion or fairness. Referees, though not obligated to do so, will allow more time for substitutions in the youth games.

Substitutions must be made through the substitution box, which is between the two teams. A player cannot come on the field until his counterpart has crossed into the substitution box unless a horn has sounded and the referee has approved a mass exchange. Time is stopped during a horn substitution.

The Officials

THERE ARE typically two officials on the field for lacrosse games. Big-time tournaments, such as the NCAA championships, will have three. Many youth leagues will get by with one, over-worked, individual.

Ahead of the game, a referee should insure that the fields are correctly lined, that playing conditions are sufficiently good, that the nets are in one piece and that each team has enough players. They must ensure that the home team has provided enough balls and a substitution horn and they must designate and instruct a timekeeper.

The NCAA guidelines insist that officials must be in place 20 minutes prior to the start of a match. This is rarely the case in youth leagues and tournaments. Many referees in youth leagues have multiple assignments in a day and must keep a tight schedule. Lacrosse games must, and usually do, start on time.

Referees have complete authority over the game, including keeping the score and the enforcement of penalties. Any discrepancy between coaches, score keepers and an official is resolved in favor of the referee. Excessive argument with a referee is considered to be unsportsmanlike behavior and can result in a penalty.

Lacrosse referees are a rare breed of individual. They are often former or current players. They may coach teams of their own, and they may play a role in the league structure. They are aggressive individuals and usually high-strung and excitable. They do not take criticism easily. Also, there are not enough of them. The sport is growing at a rate that has far outstripped the resources of the officiating staff. As a parent, never take issue with the decisions of an official. It is a no-win situation.

The Timekeeper

A SIDELINE official is in charge of keeping time. In youth lacrosse, and even at the high school level, this is often a volunteer. The officials on the field will interact throughout the game with this individual.

The timekeeper has many tasks in a lacrosse game, including keeping an account of the time in each period, keeping track of the time in the penalties, and notifying the player and coach when the penalty is over.

Additionally, the timekeeper must notify the referees at the 2 minute and 10 second left to play marks in each period. The timekeeper also has control of the horn, which allows each team to substitute on dead balls. It is the responsibility of the home team to supply the horn.

A volunteer timekeeper is in an important role and, as such, must be impartial and alert to the responsibilities of the position. Loyalties to one team or another need to be put aside and concentration on the task at hand exerted. The timekeeper cannot be caught up in the action to a point of neglecting the duties of the job.

Time

THE OFFICIAL length of time for a lacrosse game is 60 minutes, broken into 15 minute quarters and is kept by the timekeeper. If agreed by both teams, or mandated by league rules, the game may be shorter. The clock runs while the game is played and is stopped when a whistle has been blown, during a coach's time-out and at the end of a period.

A coach is allotted four time-out opportunities per game, a maximum of two per half. No time-out may exceed two minutes. If a team that called timeout is ready to resume play prior to two minutes, the referee must notify the other team who then has 20 seconds to resume play. Caring for injuries is not considered the use of a timeout unless the referee feels the team is not working efficiently to deal with the injury.

A time-out may be called while in possession of the ball, or while the ball is out of play. It must be called loudly enough for the on-field officials to hear. The timeout does not begin until the referee hears and acknowledges the time-out by blowing a whistle. Many arguments ensue in lacrosse because of failure by a referee to hear and signal a timeout, particularly when a ball or player is headed out of bounds.

During the final two minutes of the game, the team that is ahead in the score must keep the ball in their attack box once it has been entered. This is an effort to force attacking play and prevents stalling. Should the ball leave the box, it is given to the other team. If the score is tie, neither team is compelled to keep the ball in their attack area.

Over-time play, in the event of a tie is determined by the league policy. During any over-time, the role of the timekeeper and, indeed, other officials does not change.

Starting the Game

The Coin Toss

FIVE MINUTES before game time, the officials will call the captains of each team to the center of the field. The captain of the visiting team is asked to call the toss of the coin. The winner of the toss is offered an opportunity to choose between a choice of goals to begin the game or control of the first alternate possession. The losing team gets whatever the winner does not select.

To choose one goal over another is to anticipate varying field conditions affecting the game. Such a choice may be determined by adverse weather conditions.

Alternate possession is awarded in instances when the referee cannot determine possession of the ball based on ruling. Perhaps both teams were involved in a loose ball going out of bounds and the referee cannot be sure of the correct call. The ball is then given based on alternate possession. If this is the first such call in the game, the ball will go to the team that won the option in the coin toss.

The Line Up

AT THE BEGINNING of the game, the officials will have the teams assemble in a line, facing their opponents, with their left shoulder facing the goal they will be defending first. This is the opportunity for the referees to go over any rule they feel needs to be emphasized. For example, many times a referee will have the players line up 5 yards apart to demonstrate the distance they want the players to give each other after a dead ball situation.

The line up ends with each goalie coming across to the center and wishing each other luck, and then having each player wish luck to their direct opponent. The players then disperse to their starting positions for the face-off.

In the ritual of the line up, it is easy to see the tribal roots of the game of lacrosse. Some people believe that the spirits of the game watch over each contest.

The Face-off

THE GAME begins with a face-off. The referee places the ball at the center mark of the field. Two opposing mid-field players face one other. When the referee yells "DOWN," the two players go into a squatting position. Both must have their sticks four inches apart and parallel with the other, the stick heads adjacent to the ball. The other four mid-fielders will set up behind the wing area until the whistle is blown.

Next, the referee yells "SET." The players must remain motionless until the referee blows the whistle. When the whistle is blown, the two players try to "clamp" the ball or "rake" the ball to one of their midfielders. The attack and defensive players not in the mid-field area must stay in their respective box until the referee yells "POSSESSION," signaling that one or another has gained possession of the ball, if only for a moment.

Illegal procedure infractions occur often in a face-off. Players are anxious to gain possession of the ball and often make mistakes. The result of such an infraction is to award the ball to the opposing team and whistle the start of play. For instance, during the face-off, it is illegal to move before the whistle, including the wing mid-fielders. The wing mid-fielders and the face-off mid-fielder must be behind their respective lines.

In addition, a proper face-off requires that the crosses of the players be evenly matched. Both players must have both hands on the crosse. Hands may touch the ground but not the strings of the crosse. A player's feet may not touch their stick or their opponent's. The body of the player must be positioned to the left of the throat of the crosse. No portion of either crosse may touch. The body of the player cannot lean over the centerline. Once in a set position, a player must stay in that position until the whistle is blown.

Once the whistle is blown and before possession is established, it is a contest between the six mid-fielders, to the frustration of the other players on the field, who cannot move until possession. During the scrum, all of the regular rules of the game apply; such as loose ball pushes, etc.

Under certain circumstances, a second face-off will occur. This includes occurrences of the ball being sent out of bounds and the referee not able to determine who had possession, or a player losing required equipment in the center area. Perhaps an inadvertent whistle was blown. An injury may have occurred in the center area and play was stopped. Simultaneous fouls, occurring while the ball is loose, will call for a new face-off, as will a timeout that was called before there had been a possession call.

During the game, a face-off will occur at the beginning of each quarter and after each goal scored, except in certain circumstances. In youth leagues, if one team is ahead by more than a prescribed number of goals, the opposing team is given possession of the ball without a face-off under a "mercy" rule.

Also, in all leagues, if one team is in an extra man offense (man up), due to a penalty, and retained possession of the ball at the end of the previous period of play, that team begins the new period with possession of the ball, without a face-off.

Playing the Game

Penalties

AN OFFICIAL signals a rule violation by throwing a yellow flag into the air, calling loudly, "flag down." If the team that has been fouled has possession of the ball, play continues until that team loses the ball or a goal is scored. The whistle then blows, the penalty is given, the ball is returned to the team fouled or goes to a face-off, and play resumes.

Penalties are either releasable or non-releasable. The former type of penalty ends (releases), prior to expiring, when a goal is scored by the opponent of the player with the penalty. The player or a substitute may then re-enter the game. If the player never left because the other team kept possession and scored, then the penalty is expired and no time is served. Non-releasable penalties must be served in full regardless of any goals scored, and the team with the penalty continues to play without a full side of players until the penalty is served.

A player serving a penalty must remain in front of the timekeeper table for the length of the penalty. Players still serving a penalty at the end of a period must continue to serve into the next period until the penalty is over.

Penalties are of three types, personal fouls, expulsion fouls, and technical fouls. Personal fouls warrant a suspension from play for the offending player for one to three minutes depending on the judgment of the officials as to severity and intent. Personal fouls include cross checks, illegal body checks, illegal crosses, using illegal equipment, slashing, tripping, unnecessary roughness and, unsportsmanlike conduct.

Expulsion fouls are three-minutes non-releasable, and result in the player leaving the field of play for the rest of the game and being ineligible to play in the next game. Typically, an expulsion foul results from particularly vicious play or flagrant misconduct. Multiple fouls for unsportsmanlike conduct will result in expulsion. A player accumulating five personal fouls also may no longer play in the game. However, this is not an expulsion foul, and has no bearing on the next game.

Technical fouls are infractions of lesser severity than personal fouls. The penalty for a technical foul can be either a 30-second removal of the player from the game or awarding the ball to the fouled team without anyone leaving, according to the discretion of the officials. Technical fouls include crease violations, goalkeeper interference, holding, illegal offensive screens, illegal procedure (of which, there are many), conduct fouls (again, multiple types), interference, offsides, pushing, stalling, warding off and withholding the ball from play.

Certain technical fouls result in a play-on situation. The referee will clearly announce "play on" and will wait to blow the whistle based on the result of the action. Typically, if the team that has been fouled gains possession of the ball, the referee will refrain from blowing the whistle and stopping play.

In situations where a team loses a player for a length of time due to a penalty, the team finds themselves in a "man down" defense. The opponents are said to be in "extra man offense" or EMO. When the penalty is expired and the player returns to the field, the shout is "full strength".

Goals

A GOAL IS scored when the ball completely passes through the imaginary plane formed by the crossbar and the posts. The officials have complete discretion as to awarding the score. Under certain conditions, the score will not count, including if the ball goes in after the period has ended, even if the whistle has not been blown. Nor does it count if the attacking team has committed a penalty.

Should a ball enter the goal after a whistle has been blown, even if inadvertent, the score does not count. Neither does it count if an attacking player has committed a crease violation (see Crease Violation, p.50). Should the attacking team have too many men on the field or a player in an offside position, the goal is disallowed.

When a goal is scored, any releasable penalties being served by the team on which the goal is scored are released and the team returns to full strength. The referee should note the goal on his scorecard, including the number of the player who scored it.

Crease Violation

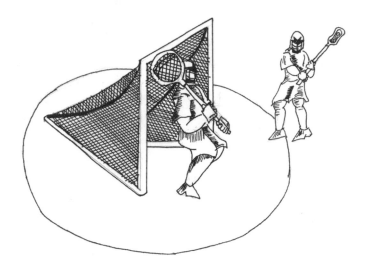

AN ATTACKING player may not touch any part of the crease, the circular area encompassing the goal, with his body or his crosse. Entering the airspace of the crease with the follow-through on a shot is legal, as long as the stick does not touch the goalie or the goalie's stick and the momentum of the player does not carry him into the crease.

Contact with the goalie, while he is in the crease area, is a crease violation. Violating the crease is a technical foul and results in a change of possession and negates any goals scored during the violation.

Defensive players, including the goalie, while in possession of the ball, have four seconds to clear themselves or the ball from inside the crease. Once outside the crease, of course, they are fair game for attack and they cannot re-enter the crease with the ball.

Goalie Privileges

WHILE IN the goal crease (his own), a goalie enjoys
certain privileges and protections as he engages
in the dangerous job of stopping shots. In order
to block a shot, the goalie may use any part of his
crosse or body, including his hands. He can not
catch the ball with his hands, but he may bat it away.
This applies to a ball that is in the crease. Touching

a ball with a hand while it is not in the crease is not allowed. So, for instance, a ball rolling into the goal may be batted away by the goalie's hand, but a ball passing through the air outside the crease cannot be.

There is no contact allowed between goalie and attacking player while the goalie is in the crease. This is regardless of possession of the ball. As noted above, the goalie has four seconds to exit the crease with the ball in his possession. If a goalie extends his stick outside the crease to attempt to get possession of the ball, the stick may be checked, however, the goalie cannot be touched while in the crease. When the goalie leaves the crease, with or without the ball, he becomes a normal player and may be legally checked.

At the restart of play in the attacking area, most referees will alert the goalie to the position of the ball before the whistle is blown. The goalie should continue to alert the defense of the ball's whereabouts as play continues. Loudly calling "top right," "x," and "top left," alerts the defense to the position of the ball.

Goalies are unique individuals, willing to take on the pressure and responsibility while braving the rejection and disappointment. It takes great courage and a significant amount of reckless abandon to play goalie in lacrosse. It is not a position for the faint of heart.

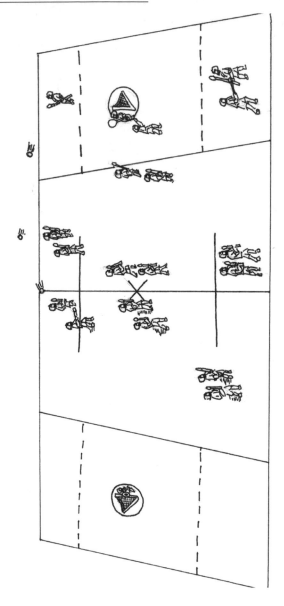

Advancing the Ball with a Clear

A PLAYER CAN throw or carry the ball down field. Throwing the ball is called a "clear." If a player gains possession of the ball in his defensive zone, he has 10 seconds to get out of the defensive zone or the ball is turned over to the other team. A player judges the time remaining in the ten seconds and either runs the ball out of the zone or clears it.

If the player is too ambitious and fails to leave the defensive zone within ten seconds, the other team gets the ball either at the spot of the violation or, if within 20 yards of the goal, at a spot twenty yards laterally from the goal. As in any turnover situation, the defensive player must give the player with the ball five yards of cushion before the whistle blows to start play.

Advancing the Ball by Cradling

CARRYING THE ball in the crosse is known as "cradling." A team with the ball has ten seconds to enter their attack zone once they have crossed the line in the center of the field. The ball must come in contact with an object, ground or player, in the area. An airborne player is not in the area if he did not leave the ground from within the area.

Having once been in the attack area, an offensive player may take the ball out of the area, assuming that the referee has not warned the team to stay in the area, such as during the final two minutes of the game. Once out of the area, a new ten seconds is applied and the offensive team has that long to advance into the area once more.

Out of Bounds

THE BALL IS OUT of bounds when it touches the end line or sideline of the field. A player is out of bounds when any part of his body or equipment touches on or outside of the boundary lines.

When a loose ball goes out of bounds, the team that touched it last loses possession of the ball to the other team. A pass out of bounds gives the same result. In the attack area, the referee will shout "pass" or "shot" based on his opinion of the intent of the player who last had the ball. If it was a "shot," the ball is given to the team who is closest to the ball when the ball went out of bounds. In the event of a tie, the ball is awarded based on alternate possession.

An airborne player is considered to be at the point he left the ground. So, should an out of bounds player leap to keep a ball in the field of play, the ball is considered out of bounds, though it may never have crossed the line. Similar logic applies to offsides situations and ten-second rules.

Parents on the sideline may have a much better view of the out of bounds player than the official on the field. An uproar will then ensue. Keep in mind that it is more important to get out of the way of the player than to contend with the official for the correct call.

Offsides

AT ALL TIMES during the game, a team must keep four defensive players on their defensive end of the field, and three offensive players on the offensive end of the field. Failing to do so is a technical foul and results in a 30-second penalty.

Often, a defensive player will consider it a good play to advance the field into the offensive end with the ball in his stick. While attempting this, another of his teammates must take his place in the defensive end. The common call heard during this play is "middie back," usually yelled excitedly by the coach and by the mid-fielder in question. If two mid-fielders remain back, it's not an offsides violation, but the offensive team is hampered by one fewer player and suffers as a result.

Swapping a defensive player for a mid-fielder in a fast-break situation is an exciting play and gives the defensive player a rare opportunity to participate in goal scoring. To execute it properly requires good communication between teammates and good lacrosse field sense. It is the mark of a well-coached team.

Fast Break

FROM AN OFFENSIVE point of view, the most exciting play in a lacrosse game is the fast break. An attacking team gains control of the ball and clears it down field faster than the defensive mid-fielders can regain their positions. The attacking team then has more men in the attacking zone than the defense. The ball moves rapidly from player to player until there is one player alone with the ball in front of the goal.

The goalkeeper must stop a point blank shot or, if quick enough, checks the player with the ball prior to a shot. Courageously defending a fast break opportunity can energize an entire team and change the momentum of a game. Well executed fast breaks are beautiful to watch.

Stalling

DURING THE LAST two minutes of regulation play, the team ahead, once in the attacking zone, must stay there. If the ball leaves the attacking zone, the ball is given to the defensive team.

If, in the opinion of the referee, a team is not trying to attack the goal, a stalling warning may be given. Should this happen, the attacking team must play within the attack zone, as though it were the last two minutes of the game.

Defensive stalling can occur. If a team leaves the defensive area with the ball but fails to attempt to cross the middle of the field, a referee may identify the play as defensive stalling. Should that happen, the referee will count loudly to five, in which time the defensive team must try to advance the ball past the middle.

A team cannot be accused of stalling if they are playing with fewer players than the opposition due to penalties.

Individual Play

A PLAYER WITH the ball runs past another with no difficulty. Another, with the poke of a stick, knocks the ball free, scoops it up and runs the other way. Someone else crashes into the player and again the ball is free. What is going on out there? Is there sense to all of this?

Dodges

WHEN A PLAYER is moving with the ball in his crosse and runs into opposition in the form of another player playing defense, he may pass the ball to a teammate or he may attempt to go past the opposing player using a technique known as a dodge. There are four clearly distinct types.

THE SPLIT DODGE involves stepping hard in one direction, inviting a stick check, then at the last moment, switching the crosse to the other hand and going in the opposite direction. The defender has committed his stick and his body in the first direction and can not compensate the other way fast enough to defend.

THE ROLL DODGE is a spin move. An offensive player will step towards the defender and spin his body and the crosse away in the opposite direction, thus evading the check.

THE FACE DODGE involves switching direction by swiping the crosse across the face of the opponent. The defender must first bite in one direction for the offensive player to succeed, otherwise the defender will check in the new direction and relieve the player of the ball. A poorly timed face dodge leaves the offensive player well exposed.

When subtlety fails, a strong, fast offensive player might employ a **BULL DODGE**. Simply stated, this ploy involves running directly into the defender with the hope of his losing his balance and ending up on the turf. This is very exciting but usually does not work very well as sticks, arms and legs often end up entangled.

Using Both Hands

MANY ASPECTS OF good lacrosse play require keeping both hands on the crosse at once. Scooping up a loose ball is best accomplished this way. One-handed checks invite penalty calls. One-handed offensive moves, similarly, draw accusations of warding off (see Warding Off, p.66) from the referee. So, it is not uncommon to hear shouts of "two hands" coming from the sidelines.

Warding Off

A PLAYER WITH possession of the ball may not use any part of his body, free hand, arm, leg, etc. to attempt to control the opponent's crosse. The player may protect the ball from the check of the opponent but may not try to alter the direction of the check by pushing the stick away. Should a referee determine that the player with the ball is warding off, the result is a technical foul. The player then relinquishes the ball to the opponent.

Defense

A LONG POLE defender has a significant advantage over an offensive player. The extended reach of the pole presents a real obstacle to retaining possession of the ball. The offensive player must use speed to counter the reach of the defender.

Midfield defenders, with short sticks, have no such advantage. The team strategy, then, is for attacking players to get past the midfield defense and create an advantage in numbers of players to defeat the long-poles inherent advantage. Quick passes then will result in shooting opportunities and, hopefully, goals.

Defense-minded players attempt to counter this by playing man to man or zone defenses as the occasion warrants and employing a teamwork device known as a slide. One player will move to fill a gap created by virtue of another player committing to checking an attacking player. To do this successfully, a defense must both anticipate each other and communicate.

It should be noted that most lacrosse games are high scoring contests. This is a clear indication of the challenge in playing good defense, as well as goalkeeping.

Checking

CHECKING, with body or stick, is fundamental to lacrosse. A correct and legal body check is executed from the side or the front above the waist and below the neck. It may be used to dislodge a ball from an opponent or to interfere with an opponent in a loose ball situation.

Similarly, a check with a crosse may be used on an opponent when in possession of the ball or in an effort to prevent gaining possession of a loose ball. This includes a ball in flight. It is then perfectly correct to hit another player's stick in order to prevent that player from catching a pass, for instance, provided the player is within five yards of the ball.

As important as checking is, there are many illegal varieties. A check to the head, from the rear, or below the waist is an immediate personal foul. However, a player is not allowed to draw a penalty by turning in a way that makes a legal check illegal. The position of the players upon initial contact is the deciding factor on the legality of the check.

Cross Check

A CHECK WITH the part of the crosse handle between the hands of the person giving the check is called a "cross check" and is illegal if extended away from the body. The hands must be together on the crosse while executing a check away from the body. The hands may be apart if the crosse is against the torso of the defender.

Spearing

A BODY CHECK involving the use of the player's head, known as "spearing," is illegal and dangerous. Body checking an opponent who is sitting, kneeling, or lying on the ground is similarly illegal. Both fouls warrant, and will receive, minimum one-minute non-releasable penalties. Severe instances will receive three-minute non-releasable penalties.

Pushing

WITH CERTAIN RESTRICTIONS, players are allowed to push one another all over the field. Pushing is defined as a non-violent blow initiated after contact has been made. It is legal from the front or the side when an opponent has the ball or is within five yards of the ball. The push must be executed by closed hand, shoulder or arm and while both hands are on the crosse.

A push not executed properly, while in a loose

ball situation, awards the ball to the opponent. A push in the back on an opponent with the ball will result in a penalty.

Holding

THERE ARE A number of ways to hinder the success of one's opponent in the course of a lacrosse game. Legal checks are the best. Several other modes of behavior are considered holding and are illegal.

A player is not allowed to step on an opponent's crosse. Neither is he allowed to hold or pin his opponent's crosse against him. He cannot use his free hand to grab his opponent, either his person or his crosse. While in possession of the ball or within five yards of the ball, an opponent may be held using the crosse. That is legal.

Defining a hold and making a call are the discretion of the referee. Severity and success are taken into account. A strong player able to play through the hold may not get a call, as the referee deems it more in the interest of the game to ignore it and continue.

Interference

THE INTERFERENCE penalty involves action against a player by another when that player is not in possession of the ball or is not within five yards of a loose ball. An illegal offensive screen, for instance, one in which the player setting the screen continues moving, is considered interference. This is analogous to a moving pick in the game of basketball.

Stepping into the path of a cutting attack man, to bar his way in front of the goal, is interference. Hitting or pushing a player nowhere near the play is interference at a minimum, and perhaps unnecessary roughness (see Unnecessary Roughness, p.82). It is not legal, then, to shove an attacking player away from the front of the goal, as it is in ice hockey.

Accidental or extraneous contact with a player

is only interference if the player was involved in the play and the player who initiated the contact was attempting to hamper his participation in the play. The referee makes the judgment based on the run of play. For instance, a defense player watching the flight of a pass moves into another position and right into an attacking player. Neither player is guilty of interference, as the play was away from them both and neither was impeded for long.

Slashing

SLASHING IS A common personal foul in a lacrosse match. It is illegal to swing a crosse with reckless abandon in an attempt to strike a player possessing the ball. Nor is a check of deliberate viciousness allowed. The referee is within the rules to call slashing on a legitimate check based on evidence of ferocity.

Repeated blows to the body, particularly after a warning has been issued, are considered deliberately violent. Strictly speaking, any blow to the body of an opponent is a slash. However, if that opponent is using his body to protect the crosse and the ball in it, then the blow is not a slash.

At all times, a blow to the head or the neck, while attempting to dislodge the ball, is a slash. The contact must be a blow, however. Grazing the head or face is considered a brush. Should the defensive player's crosse be pushed upward to the head of the player by that player's arm or crosse, it is not a slash.

Tripping

DURING THE course of a game, many players fall many times. Most are a normal and legitimate result of the action. Now and then, however, players get a little help from their opponent.

It is against the rules to deliberately impede a player below the waist, causing them to fall, if standing, or struggle to get up, if already fallen. A correct check that causes a crosse to fall and trip it's owner is not a penalty.

Unnecessary Roughness

THE REFEREE IS in a position to decide if play is of too violent a nature, and may penalize a player for unnecessary roughness should that be the case. This includes checks that could have been avoided but instead ended up being violent and deliberate.

In particular, a check may not be delivered in a punching manner, regardless if the hand is on the crosse. A late hit on an offensive player, after a shot has been taken, is another instance of unnecessary roughness. Unnecessary roughness is a qualitative penalty and is a means to keep the level of play fair and within bounds.

Unsportsmanlike Conduct

The rules of lacrosse prohibit anyone from arguing with, or attempting to influence, an official. No one associated with the lacrosse team is allowed to use obscene, profane, or threatening language or gestures during a game. This includes fans, and school staff and administration.

Doing so is a violation of the rules for conduct and results in a penalty. Repeated violations add up to the five penalty expulsion criteria. In addition, taunting, excessive celebration, and other acts of poor sportsmanship are against the rules and may be penalized according to severity.

Three other actions also constitute unsportsmanlike conduct. A player may not repeatedly commit the same technical foul. A player leaving the field of play legally may not delay returning to the field, and a substitute must follow the rules for entering the field of play. Otherwise, these players will face penalties for unsportsmanlike conduct.

Other Rules and Regulations

Play Stoppage

IF A BALL gets stuck in mud on the field or lodged in equipment, the referee will stop play to free the ball and award it on an alternative possession basis. A ball that has been caught in the side netting of the goal will be given to the defense outside of the defensive area.

A coach may stop play and request a count of long-pole defenders at any time during the game. However, if a coach has made such a request twice and both times it is shown that the legal number of long-pole defenders are on the field, the team making the request will be charged a technical foul.

Illegal Procedure

ILLEGAL PROCEDURE defines a broad list of technical fouls. Each is eligible for a 30-second releasable penalty. Examples of illegal procedure include failing to give a player the required five yard cushion when restarting play, playing without a crosse, playing with a broken crosse, and flicking a crosse into the face of an opponent.

Showing up late, if avoidable, will warrant an illegal procedure penalty.

Failures by the home team to live up to its

responsibilities, such as notifying the visiting team of a late start or not having enough balls are illegal procedures

Failing to advance out of the defensive area in ten seconds, and deliberately creating a loose ball situation in order to avoid the ten-second rule are both forms of illegal procedure, as is attempting to fake a penalty by taking a dive, or pretending to receive a blow to the head (which could possibly be an unsportsmanlike penalty as well).

Conduct Fouls

CONDUCT FOULS are rule violations generated from outside the field of play by official personnel of a team. They include restricting the coach's area to the coaches. No one else is allowed there during the game. No coach is allowed on the field during the game other than to address an injury or to warm-up a goalie at half time.

Using electronic aids to communicate with players on the field is illegal and a conduct foul. Placing noise-making groups, such as school bands or rooting clubs behind the opposition is a conduct foul. The most often occurring conduct foul, however, is objecting to an official's decision.

Resuming Play

To RESUME PLAY, the referee gives the ball to a player on the team to whom he has awarded posession. The referee will then see that the player with the ball is on the field of play ("Step in, please.") and that the opposition is at least five yards away. He will then blow the whistle, and play begins.

After a ball has gone out-of-bounds, the starting position will be the point it was last on the field. When a foul has occurred, with penalty time to be served and it happened in the defensive end of the field, the re-start will take place with a mid-fielder at the middle of the field. If there was no penalty time given, the re-start happens at the point of the whistle or 20 yards laterally of the goal.

Team Penalties

WHEN A PENALTY occurs that is not given to an identified player but to the team as a whole, the penalty time is served by the designated "In-Home," the first attack player on the roster. This player must be a starting player. It is he, who will serve the penalty and be shown to have done so on the scorecard. The penalty counts towards his five allowable penalties. Two team penalties will be served by the "In-Home" and the adjacent attack player named on the starting roster.

Dead Ball Fouls

DEAD BALL FOULS are penalties occurring after play has stopped. Perhaps a player retaliates for a slash with one of his own, or another individual argues the justice of the call that stopped play and receives a conduct penalty. These are dead ball fouls and time is served beginning with the resumption of play.

Simultaneous Fouls

FOULS COMMITTED by both teams are ruled to be simultaneous. However, the judgment of the severity, according to time to be served, will determine who gets the ball. If the arithmetic shows one team to be penalized with less time than the other, that team will begin play in possession of the ball. If all fouls are technical fouls or if the penalty time assessed is equal, then the ball goes to either the team that had possession, or, if neither team did, the team due the ball with the next alternate possession.

Slow Whistle

ONCE A PENALTY by a defense is signaled with a flag down, the attacking team may continue to attack until such time as a goal is scored, the defense gains control of the ball, the ball is knocked loose or the ball goes out of bounds. The whistle then blows and the penalty assessed. The ball is returned to the attacking team if a goal was not scored, or to a face-off if it was.

Should a goal be scored during a slow whistle situation, any penalty for personal foul violations will still be served. A technical foul penalty will be waived off.

Play-On

A LOOSE BALL technical foul or a crease violation may, if the whistle is blown immediately, result in a disadvantaged situation for the team that was fouled, since the re-start would happen at the point of the foul. In such a case, the referee will signal "play on" and will wait to see who gains control of the ball. If the team that was fouled wins the ball, play continues. If the fouling team wins the ball, the whistle blows and possession is awarded to the other team.

The End of Play

Shaking Hands

IT IS CUSTOMARY and expected for each team to line up on the field at the end of play, usually with the goalie in front and the coaches and trainers in the back. Each team advances towards the other, passing on the left and offers the opponents congratulations on a game well played, regardless of the outcome or any ill feelings generated by the game. A team that will not do this is not a team with which to be associated.

Web Sites

THE WORLD OF lacrosse has embraced
the Internet. There are many interesting and
informative sites. Below, please find some good
starting points for filling any gaps this guide has
left in understanding and detail. Search engines will
yield even more.

USLacrosse
http://www.uslacrosse.org/

LaxLinks
http://www.laxlinks.com/

National Lacrosse League
http://www.nll.com/

Major League Lacrosse League
http://www.majorleaguelacrosse.com/

Inside Lacrosse
http://www.insidelacrosse.com/

Living Traditions—Lacrosse
http: //www.virtualmuseum.ca/Exhibitions/
Traditions/English/lacrosse_ref.html

English Lacrosse Association
http: //www.englishlacrosse.co.uk/2004/index.html

Camps

A PLAYER SHOULD attend a good camp in his early teens to learn the game, make friends and absorb the culture. If a player aspires to play for a particular college, a camp at that school provides excellent exposure.

Lacrosse camps are located throughout the US and Canada. An Internet search will provide comprehensive information on many of them. The following camps are well known to the author and are highly recommended. Excellent camps are to be found associated with other schools, as well.

Hogan's Camps at the University of Pennsylvania:
University of Pennsylvania
235 S. 33rd Street
Dunning Coaches' Center
Philadelphia, PA 19104
(215) 898-6127
www.hoganscamps.com

Syracuse Men's Lacrosse Camp
Manley Field House
Syracuse, NY 13244-5020
(315) 443-4390

Lacrosse Camp at the University of Virginia
2635 Meriwether Drive
Charlottesville, VA 22901

Princeton Lacrosse Camp
Princeton, NJ
Contact: Bill Tierney at tierney@princeton.edu
(609) 258-3369

To order additional copies of this book:

Please send a check or money order for $16.95 ($22.95 Canadian) plus $3.50 shipping and handling ($5.25 shipping to Canada) per copy to:

3G Productions, Inc.
P. O. Box 1310
Doylestown, PA 18901

Pennsylvania residents, please add 6% sales tax.

A Sideline Guide to Boy's Lacrosse is available to organizations at a bulk discount. Please contact David Wilbur at djwilbur@hwico.com or (215) 962-5682 for more information. Minimum order to qualify for bulk discount is 25 books.

About the Author

THE AUTHOR, David Wilbur, is the father of three male lacrosse players and one, female, soccer player. He has logged thousands of miles, watched hundreds of lacrosse games in both fair weather and foul. Years of discussion on the sideline have confirmed the general confusion among the game's greatest supporters. This book is his effort to share what he has learned. He lives with his family in Bucks County, PA, an up-and-coming hotbed of lacrosse.